Poopy Science

Getting to the Bottom of What Comes Out Your Bottom

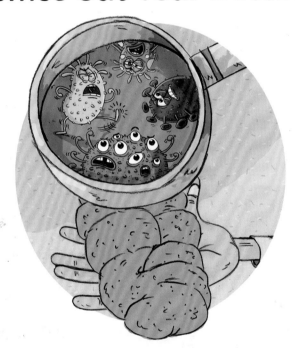

Written by **Edward Kay**

Illustrated by **Mike Shiell**

KIDS CAN PRESS

To Be Is to Do Doo-Doo

The book that you are holding in your hands, possibly even while sitting on the toilet reading it, will tell you everything from A to Z about going number 1 and 2. It's a veritable manual of manure, and a primer on pee. Make no mistake: body waste grosses everybody out. But it's a natural part of life, something that all organisms have to do in order to live. In fact, the waste cycle is an important part of our planet's ecology. So get ready to become an expert in excreta, a litterateur of the latrine! Just don't forget to wash your hands with soap and water!

Contents

The Scoop on Poop!

There's no stepping over the facts: most people are totally disgusted by poop and pee, also known as excreta. Every human culture in the world finds excreta revolting and has *taboos* around it. In the Old Testament of the Bible, the Israelites are warned not to leave their poop lying around but to bury it outside their camp instead, lest God get offended and "turn away" from them. The ancient Egyptians very sensibly had strict rules about not eating poop. (But then again, they also worshipped dung beetles.) Now, just saying some of the words that we have created for excreta is considered bad manners.

So why do we find our own waste so icky? Psychologists believe it's an instinctive human reaction to harmful things, just like other animals are instinctively afraid of fire. For us, those harmful things include the **hepatitis** virus and germs found in poop, such as *E. coli* and **salmonella**, all of which can make us very sick or even kill us. Also on that list are some truly hideous **parasites**, such as tapeworms and pinworms, that live in human bowels and can be transferred through contact with an infected person's poop. *Eww!* So to protect ourselves, we have evolved to find the look and smell of poop nauseating, just like we are nauseated by the odor of spoiled milk or rotting meat.

Stinky Stool

The reason you can smell that foul fecal odor is that tiny turd bits are actually floating up your nose to your scent receptors! Sorry, but that's the truth.

A **molecule** is the smallest physical unit of a substance. In the case of an element, the molecule is made up of two or more of the same type of atoms. Meanwhile, in a compound, the molecule consists of two or more different types of atoms. While there's no such thing as a poop molecule, there are molecules of other chemicals that, when we smell them together, make the odor we recognize as poop.

One of the molecules that create that icky smell is a substance called mercaptan. It is made up of atoms of carbon, hydrogen and sulfur and looks like this:

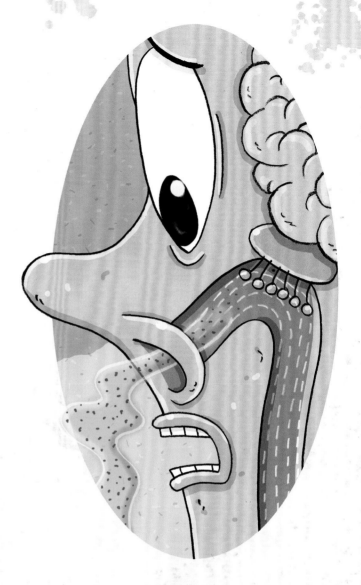

Indole is another type of chemical found in poop. Indole molecules look like this:

Together, mercaptan and indole make that familiar funky smell.

We dislike feces so much that there's even a word for the fear of poop or pooping: *coprophobia*.

Can't Live with It, Can't Live without It

Though we may find it revolting, excreta has played a major role in human civilization. Wars have been fought with it and over it. Our bodies couldn't function without making it and getting rid of it. In fact, if you live to be 80 years old, you will produce approximately 11 t (25 000 lb.) of poop — that's about the weight of a bus! Luckily, you don't have to poop it all out at the same time. On average, you pee enough every year to fill two bathtubs — though we don't recommend you pee in any bathtubs to prove it!

Even though excreta is not only gross but potentially dangerous, it can come in handy — and not just if you're a captive chimpanzee, an animal that sometimes throws its poop at annoying zoo visitors. As you'll see later in this book, poop and pee have many uses beyond just getting rid of things we don't want in our bodies.

How Sweet It Is!

Not all creatures produce excreta that smells or tastes bad. Some organisms, such as yeast, eat the sugars in grape juice and poop out alcohol. That helps make the fine wines that connoisseurs love to swirl around in their mouths and describe as having flavors of "wet dog," "pencil shavings" and "cat pee."

Your 11 t (25 000 lb.) of feces might sound like a lot, but it's nothing compared to what the blue whale can poo! It can excrete up to 3 t (6600 lb.) of poop per day. Blue whales can live up to 90 years, so over its lifetime, it can create about 98 550 t (217 million lb.) of feces. That's about the same weight as a 140 m (450 ft.) cargo ship!

The Scoop on *Your* Poop

Poop and pee are the unavoidable by-products of eating and drinking. Here's why your body produces them: when you eat, powerful digestive juices in your stomach and intestines break the food down so that your body can absorb the nutrients it needs, such as *proteins, carbohydrates, fats, vitamins* and *minerals*. The parts that your body can't absorb, such as fiber, are pushed through to the colon (the end of your digestive system). Your poop is about 75 percent water. The rest is fiber, dead and living gut bacteria, mucus from the lining of your intestines and dead cells that your body is shedding.

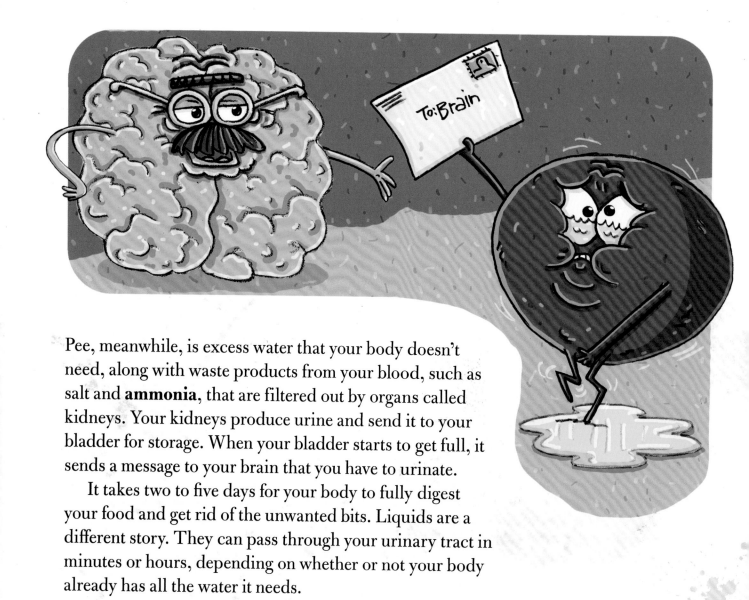

Pee, meanwhile, is excess water that your body doesn't need, along with waste products from your blood, such as salt and **ammonia**, that are filtered out by organs called kidneys. Your kidneys produce urine and send it to your bladder for storage. When your bladder starts to get full, it sends a message to your brain that you have to urinate.

It takes two to five days for your body to fully digest your food and get rid of the unwanted bits. Liquids are a different story. They can pass through your urinary tract in minutes or hours, depending on whether or not your body already has all the water it needs.

Digestive System

When you smell something tasty, your mouth makes saliva.

Your teeth, plus enzymes in your saliva, break down your food so you can swallow it.

The food moves down your esophagus to your stomach.

Your stomach's muscles and acidic juices break down the food even smaller.

Chemicals in your small intestine break it down even further so your body can get the nutrients it needs.

Those nutrients are absorbed by your blood, and carried to your liver, where harmful substances are filtered out.

The unusable parts of your food, such as fiber, are passed on to your large intestine.

Your body absorbs minerals and water, turning what it can't use into poop. The poop moves to the rectum, where it waits for your next bowel movement.

Your digestive system is about 9 m (30 ft.) long — almost the same length as a telephone pole!

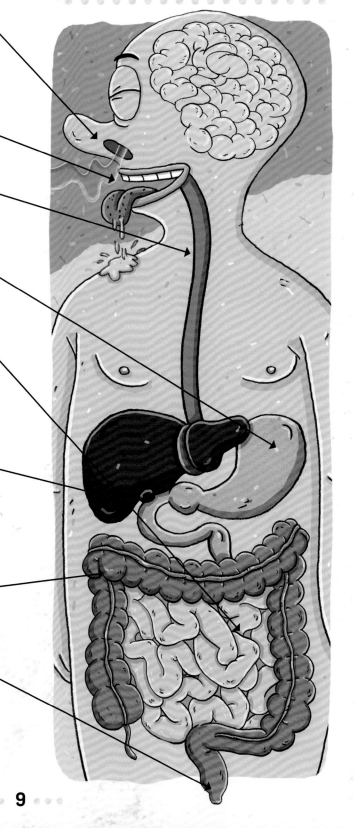

Berry Scary

In 1971, thousands of worried parents brought their children to hospitals, fearing that they were bleeding internally because their poop was bright red. Fortunately, the children were fine. The culprit was Franken Berry, a breakfast cereal colored with dyes that made poop scarlet.

That was a false alarm, but sometimes your poop's color *can* reveal health problems. If yours is suddenly red, yellow, black or green, it might be a harmless reaction to beets, licorice, leafy vegetables, vitamins, medicines or food colorings — or it could be a medical issue. If in doubt, ask a parent or caregiver.

The texture of your poop can also tell you important things about your health. Normally, poop is soft and sausage shaped. If you're constipated (having bowel movements fewer than four times a week), your feces will be hard and lumpy. That's because the longer poop stays in your intestines, the more water your body draws out of it. To avoid constipation, exercise regularly, drink plenty of fluids and eat high-fiber foods, such as fruits, vegetables and whole grains. Fiber "tickles" your innards, contracting your bowel muscles and keeping waste moving.

Normally, urine ranges from pale yellow to amber. But it can be bright yellow, reddish or even bluish. As with poop, unusual colors in your pee could be a sign of illness or just the result of something that you ate or drank.

Too Mush of a Good Thing

Diarrhea is runny poop. Sometimes sugar, sugar substitutes, fried or fatty foods, dairy products, wheat, barley and even some medicines can cause diarrhea. So can bacteria, viruses and parasites, especially when you're in a new place where your immune system doesn't know any of the germs yet. Normally, your white blood cells recognize and destroy germs that get inside you. Your blood also produces special proteins called **antibodies** that attach themselves to germs and signal more white blood cells to attack. But if you've never encountered a particular germ before, it'll take time for your immune system to recognize the invader. In the meantime, you'll feel very ill. The best way to avoid getting traveler's diarrhea is to eat only cooked foods, drink bottled water and avoid ice cubes. And whether you're at home or abroad, remember to wash your hands and clean raw fruits and vegetables before eating them.

In ancient China, doctors checked on the emperor's health by smelling his poop. Luckily for your family physician, modern fecal and urine analysis can reveal medical problems without a sniff test.

Feeling Blue? Try Poo!

Don't look now, but you've got company. *Trillions* of guests, in fact. They are tiny organisms, or microbes, known as **gut microbiota**, and they do important things for you, such as helping you digest your food and absorb nutrients.

Medical researchers believe that some of these gut microbes can even affect our moods and eating habits. Some might cause depression. Some might make us want to eat fatty, unhealthy foods. Microbes like *C. difficile* can make us sick or even kill us.

But other microbes might help us fight diseases, keep us happy or make us crave healthy foods. Scientists are experimenting with replacing harmful microbes with ones that can help us. And how do they do this? Glad you asked: through a poop transplant. Yes, doctors take poop from a healthy person and insert it into the bowels of someone who is sick, depressed or dangerously overweight. The idea is that **beneficial** microbes in the healthy, happy poop will reproduce in their new home, crowd out the bad microbes and make the sick person healthy and happy, too.

If you're tempted to offer your poo to a friend who is blue, be aware that doctors caution us not to try this at home. Just like operating a nuclear reactor or flying a supersonic jet, poop transplants are best left to the professionals!

A doctor who specializes in medical issues related to the rectum is called a proctologist. The ancient Egyptians held proctologists in high regard and called them the "shepherds of the anus."

Poop Soup?

Believe it or not, the idea of a "poop transplant" dates back to fourth-century China, when a doctor named Ge Hong created a diarrhea treatment called "yellow soup." It was a broth made from the dried or **fermented** poop of a healthy person. After the sick person drank the broth, the beneficial bacteria from the healthy person's feces would multiply inside the sick person's stomach, making them well. It was a simple yet ingenious solution to a serious problem. But don't look for it on your supermarket shelves. For some reason, poop soup never really caught on with people the way chicken noodle did.

What to Do with All That Poo?

When there were relatively few humans on Earth, they could poop freely as they roamed around in search of game, nuts and berries — without worrying about cleaning up after themselves. Their waste would eventually be consumed by animals and microbes and recycled as nutrients. But as humans began living together in towns and cities, and evacuating their bowels in the same places all the time, nature couldn't keep up with our inclination toward defecation. People were confronted with a vexing question: What do we do with all that poo? Because even a healthy person's feces are full of dangerous germs such as *E. coli*, a bacteria that can cause severe stomach cramps and diarrhea. Or there are parasites like pinworms that can lay thousands of eggs in you, make your bum very itchy and are just generally disgusting. So getting rid of large amounts of feces is an important problem.

Sanitation for the Nation

The history of the potty is spotty. Archaeologists' best guess is that **latrines** drained by water into pits were invented about 4000 years ago by both the Minoans in present-day Crete and the Harappans in present-day Pakistan and northern India.

During the first millennium BCE, the Greeks developed public latrines as well as non-flushing toilets in private homes. A few hundred years later, the Romans took it to a whole new level. They built a vast empire. And vast empires produce vast amounts of poop! So the Romans built communal toilets and sewer systems with underground pipes that used water to wash human waste into nearby rivers.

To Wipe or Not to Wipe

To clean their butts after pooping, the Romans used a sponge on a stick. Known as a tersorium, it was shared by everyone using the public toilets, so it got revoltingly grungy. After wiping their bums with the tersorium, Romans would clean the sponge with vinegar and water. *Yuck!* Besides being messy and unpleasant, a poopy sponge on a stick is an ideal breeding ground for bacteria.

To the east, the Chinese were developing a more hygienic method of bum wiping, now known to us and our derrieres as toilet paper. The Chinese made the first toilet paper out of bamboo and cotton rags. The earliest reference to this is in the texts of a scholar named Yen Chih-Thui, who advised that paper with important quotations should not be used to wipe your behind. With or without quotations, toilet paper was considered a luxury item reserved only for royal bums until around the fourteenth century.

Sanitation Goes Down the Drain

Unfortunately, just as European civilization was figuring out what to do with its excreta, along came a period now known as the Dark Ages. Germanic tribes who didn't give a toot about plumbing — or wiping their bums with sponges on sticks — conquered Rome. The government collapsed, wars broke out between rival kingdoms, people fled the cities and the population declined. In such turbulent circumstances, much of the knowledge that the Greeks and Romans had acquired over centuries was lost, including knowledge of sanitation.

For example, in medieval London, the sewer system built by the Romans fell into disuse. Instead, Londoners, like other Europeans, began dumping their sewage in filthy pits or simply emptying their chamber pots into the streets. This gave England's capital a very nasty odor and made it a breeding ground for germs.

Improvements in sanitation were gradual. The first flush toilet was invented in England by Sir John Harington in 1596, around the same time that William Shakespeare wrote *Romeo and Juliet*. Harington's system used gravity to release a whopping 28 L (7½ gal.) of water from a tank above the toilet. That water flushed feces away into pipes, which in turn carried it to a vault. From there, it's not clear where Harington thought the poop would go, but it didn't really matter. Because while Shakespeare became world famous, Harington made one toilet for Queen Elizabeth I, and that was more or less the end of the line for his invention. It would be a few more centuries until flush toilets achieved widespread popularity.

Crappy Nappies

You likely don't remember when you wore diapers, but whoever changed yours probably does. In premodern times, parents and other baby minders had to make do with whatever was available, including animal skins, cloths and leaves. The first recorded use of the word *diaper* to describe baby-butt coverings was in England in 1590. Diapers must have caught on quickly, because Flemish artist Adriaen Brouwer recorded diaper changing in his 1631 painting *Unpleasant Duties of a Father*, showing a grimacing dad wiping the bum of his offspring.

Flaming Farts and Exploding Excreta!

In the late eighteenth century, a period known as the Industrial Revolution began. Technology rapidly advanced and factories sprang up in the cities. As people moved from the country, looking for work, urban populations grew rapidly … and so did the amount of poop they made. But nobody gave much thought to safely getting rid of all that excreta. Some was stored in cesspits, then hauled away by people called gong farmers, who sold the "night soil" to real farmers for use as fertilizer. But the cesspits were often leaky, so germs from feces got into the water supply and made people ill.

Ironically, when flush toilets became popular, they made the situation worse, because now feces and filthy water was pumped straight from toilets through the sewers and into rivers. The first toilets had other glitches, too. Deep in the sewers, decomposing poop created combustible gases such as ammonia, **methane** and **hydrogen sulfide**, which rose up through the pipes and into homes, like a giant explosive fart! At that time, homes were lit with candles and lamps, so when sewer gases reached those open flames, a lot of people got a bigger bang out of the new invention than they'd bargained for!

One Great Stink

In London, the population doubled between 1800 and 1850, making it the largest city in the world. Untreated sewage leached into drinking water supplies and caused cholera outbreaks that killed more than 30 000 people. Things got even worse in the hot summer of 1858, when the stench of feces in the Thames River became so bad that members of parliament feared that the vapors would kill them. The incident became known as "the Great Stink."

Since many people got their drinking water from the Thames River, it was a truly disgusting situation. Apparently, this was just the inspiration that politicians needed to finally do something. They commissioned an engineer named Joseph Bazalgette to create the first modern sewer system. When it was completed, toilets flushed waste and water into a network of over 2000 km (1240 mi.) of underground sewers, where giant pumps moved it downriver, past the city, through massive outflow pipes and into the sea. Bazalgette even solved the exploding sewer-gas problem! He routed it up above the streets through 9 m (30 ft.) iron tubes that Londoners dubbed "stink pipes."

Paleo Poop

Even when painters aren't around to immortalize historical poop events, researchers can tell a lot about our ancestors' diets and health by examining the poop they left behind, known as **paleofeces**. Paleofeces are actual poop, preserved through a natural chemical process where sugars in the feces form a hard casing that preserves the turd lurking beneath.

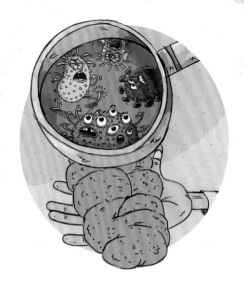

The Proof Is in the Poop

Larger objects in paleofeces, such as seeds, are visible to the naked eye. Others, such as parasite eggs, can be seen through a microscope. **DNA** analysis of paleofeces reveals what types of foods the paleopooper ate. For example, researchers have learned that Neanderthals, who lived from about 130 000 to 40 000 years ago, had a healthy diet consisting of fruit, vegetables and meat.

Paleofeces also reveal that the ancient Greeks and Romans suffered from gut parasites, a result of fertilizing their crops with untreated raw sewage. Particles found in the *Mayflower* colonists' paleofeces show that while they may have enjoyed turkey for Thanksgiving, they were also unwittingly chowing down on beetles, which had snuck into their ship's food supplies.

Studying paleofeces for things such as pollen can also reveal what the climate was like and what plants were growing where and when the poop was made. Researchers are careful when poking around in ancient turds, however, because dangerous viruses and bacteria can survive for hundreds and even thousands of years.

Living Large

The largest human paleopoop ever found is known as the Lloyds Bank turd, so called because it was unearthed on the site of a branch of the bank in York, United Kingdom, where a Viking settlement once stood. It measures about 20 cm (8 in.) long and 5 cm (2 in.) across. Scientists who examined it concluded that its Viking creator ate meat, grains and vegetables — but didn't chew carefully, because it also contains a complete, undigested hazelnut! They also suffered from a particularly horrid intestinal worm called *Ascaris lumbricoides*. It causes stomach pain and diarrhea and can migrate through the human body, sometimes emerging through its victim's eyes. If you want to see this historically significant turd for yourself, it's on display at the JORVIK Viking Centre in York.

Species and Feces

Animals poop and pee for the same biological reasons we do.
But many of them also use their excreta to send each other messages.
(Tip: Don't try this with your friends, teachers and classmates.
Stick to texting and email.)

As you may have noticed, dogs pee (and pee and pee …) to mark "their" territory. Some male dogs strain on their tippy-toes to pee as high as they can to trick other dogs into thinking they're bigger than they are.

European badgers live in groups and dig rectangular poop pits, letting other badgers know that the area is already taken by strong, well-fed badgers — so scram!

Tigers make piles of poop called scrapes to mark their territory and warn wandering rivals.

River otters are experts at smelly signals. They flatten the vegetation along a riverbank, then use it as a giant latrine, creating a poop field that can be seen — and smelled — by rival otters.

Get a Whiff of This!

Many animals can tell the sex, age and health of another animal just by sniffing its poop or pee. Some animals actually use excreta to attract a partner. (Here's another tip: it doesn't work with humans.) For example, cats let other cats know they're ready to mate by spraying urine. For the Egyptian vulture, nothing says romance like a steaming pile of yellow cow dung. Why? Because the yellowest poop contains carotenoids, vitamins found in carrots and other vegetables. If you're a vulture, carotenoids turn your beak an irresistible shade of yellow to help you attract a mate — and turn rival vultures green with envy.

The wombat, an Australian **marsupial**, is unique among animals in that it uses powerful muscles inside its bowels to shape its poop into cubes, which it stacks up to mark its territory and attract mates. Scientists aren't sure why wombats have evolved this way, except that it might be easier for them to stack square turds than round ones. It remains a marsupial mystery ...

Male giraffes figure out if female giraffes are ready to mate by nuzzling their rear ends until the female pees. Then the male takes a sip of the urine, allowing him to detect the chemicals that signal whether she is raring to reproduce.

Poopy Protection

While many animals use excreta to say, "Hey world, here I am!" some use it to avoid being noticed. If you have a dog, you might have seen it roll in another animal's feces. This stinky instinct may be a holdover from the days when their ancestors were predators. Some scientists think that rolling in the poop of a plant-eating animal masks a dog's scent, allowing it to sneak up on its victim without being sniffed out.

While some animals use poop to prey, others employ doo-doo deterrents on their would-be predators. The dwarf sperm whale, for example, has a very unappetizing way of persuading hungry orcas and sharks to look for a meal elsewhere. When threatened, the whale empties its bowels in their faces, releasing up to 11 L (3 gal.) of liquid fecal matter — in other words, defensive diarrhea! The whale then thrashes the water with its tail to stir it all up, giving the attacker a face full of poop soup. It's such an unappealing first course that would-be diners quickly lose their appetite.

Unlike the whale, a bird known as the double-banded courser uses *other* animals' poop to foil predators. It makes its nest on the ground and hides its eggs in plain sight, laying them close to antelope droppings, which are very similar in shape, size and color. Predators think the eggs are dung and leave them alone.

To attract a mate, male hippos swish their tails around while pooping, flinging their feces all over the nearest female that takes their fancy. If she is attracted to him, she will show that the feces are mutual by flinging her poop onto him in return. Talk about a bridal shower!

Funky Frass

The swallowtail butterfly caterpillar goes a step further and disguises *itself* as poop to avoid being eaten. Its splotchy black-and-white coloring looks just like bird droppings. Meanwhile, skipper butterfly caterpillars prevent predators from sniffing out their homes by flinging their tiny turds (or frass, as they're known) a distance nearly the human equivalent of a football field. Not even the best player in the NFL can manage that! Well, NFL players only throw footballs, not their poo (at least we hope they don't), but you get the point. In an even more devious case of dung deception, a caterpillar known as the fall armyworm poops onto the leaves of corn plants to trick them into thinking they're being attacked by **fungus**. Why? The corn plant can defend itself against only one kind of attacker at a time, so as it prepares a chemical **deterrent** against what it thinks is fungus, it leaves itself vulnerable to the very hungry caterpillar.

Super-Duper Poopers and Tiny Turd Makers

Animal poop comes in all sizes and shapes. Can you guess which poop belongs to which animal? By the end of this section, you'll be an excreta expert. Here's a clue: large animals usually make large poop!

Blue whale poop is important to the environment. When the whales return from feeding in deep water, they poop near the surface, releasing nutrients that feed phytoplankton. Besides providing food for other sea creatures, phytoplankton absorb carbon from the atmosphere, lessening the effects of climate change.

Manure Matchup: Which Poop Is Which?

1. Elephants make 70 kg (155 lb.) of poop every day!

2. Blue whales create cloudy poop trails that are 20 m (65 ft.) long. That's about the length of two school buses!

3. Flies and spiders leave tiny droppings. If you look closely, you can sometimes spot them in the corners of windows.

4. Cows and other herbivores that drink a lot of water make large, wet patties.

5. Sheep and other animals that get their moisture from grass and other plants have dry, pellet-like poop.

6. Wolves have tubular-shaped poop that often contains hair and bone fragments from the animals they've eaten.

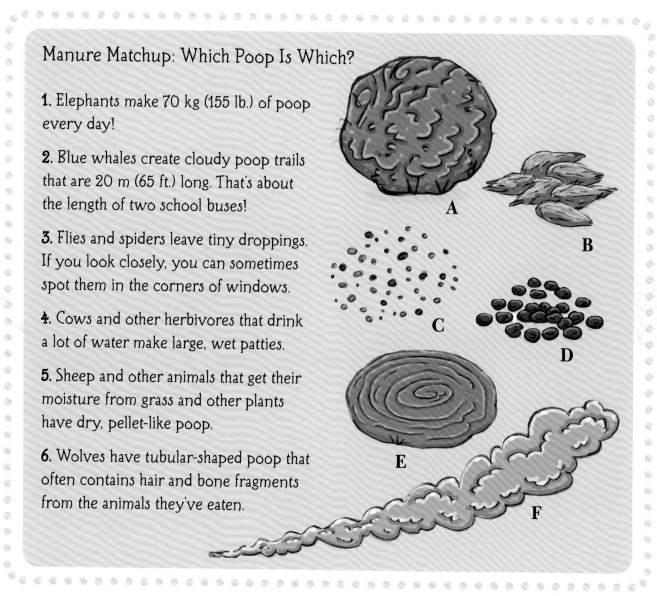

The Most Efficient Pooper

Birds have evolved to poop and pee at the same time. They have one orifice, the cloaca, that does both jobs. So, if you get splattered by a bird answering nature's call, don't think of it as getting pooped on. Think of it as getting peed on, too! On the bright side, birds don't have long intestines where stinky gases can build up, so you'll never have to worry about a bird farting on you!

Speaking of bird turds, many plants rely on birds to reproduce. When birds poop out undigested seeds, they help new plants grow in areas where they're not competing with their parents. The turds even provide the seedlings with fertilizer.

Poopy Paradise

If you ever have the chance to bask on Hawaii's famous white sand beaches … well, congratulations, you've just frolicked on a whole lot of fish poop! Those sandy beaches are the by-products of parrotfish, who feed on algae by scraping it off dead coral with their beaks. While doing so, they ingest some of the coral skeletons, which are made of a hard chemical compound called calcium carbonate. The parrotfish can't digest the skeletons, so they get ground up and pooped out as sand. Just one parrotfish produces hundreds of pounds of sand every year, ensuring those famous beaches stay as sandy and white as … poop. Parrotfish poop, that is!

A Feast of Feces

As unappealing as it sounds — and it sounds *very* unappealing — animals engage in a veritable culinary Olympics of poop munching! If someone were to give out awards for poop, here's who might be among the champions.

Sweetest Poop: Aphids

Most Recycled Poop: Rabbits

Aphid poop is better known as honeydew. It's mostly excess sugar that aphids excrete after sucking sap from plants. And ants love to eat that sweet honeydew poop, just like humans like to eat maple syrup. Except that luckily for us, maple syrup does not travel through a bug's butt on the way to our pancakes.

Rabbits actually eat their *own* poop. And it's not sugar poop. It's poop poop. Why? Because rabbits aren't able to completely digest their food the first time around. Therefore, they don't get all of the nutrients out of it. So they munch on their droppings to get the nourishment they missed.

Family-Friendliest Poop: Pandas

Grossest Dining Habits: Marabou Storks

Panda cubs eat their parents' poop to get the gut bacteria they need to digest their food. Aren't you glad you're not a panda?

These storks from sub-Saharan Africa have even grosser eating habits than your little brother. Also known as the "undertaker bird," because of its fondness for eating stinky dead things, the marabou stork is also happy to chow down on — wait for it — human feces.

Manure-Munching Champ: Dung Beetles

When dung is actually your first name, you know you're special. Unlike rabbits, dung beetles prefer munching on other animals' feces. They love it so much, they even lay their eggs in it, so that when their babies are born, they'll have a tasty, nutritious meal waiting for them. It might seem disgusting, but it's a very successful survival strategy. Dung beetles live on every continent except Antarctica.

The marabou stork's love affair with poop doesn't end there. It also defecates on its own legs to stay cool! Its white feces act like a heat shield for its black legs.

Dung Detectives

Many animals are shy and difficult to observe in the wild. Fortunately, their scat is not nearly so bashful. By studying it, researchers can tell which species live in a given area, how many there are, whether they are healthy or not and, through DNA analysis, even whether they are related to each other. Scat can also tell a lot about an animal's diet. Herbivore droppings have undigested plant material in them. Feces from predators, such as wolves and owls, contain bones, fur, feathers and other things they can't digest. Birds often leave plant seeds behind in their messy droppings.

Do wild bears poop in the woods? Not if they're hibernating. When they bed down for the winter, bears create a fecal plug to block their butts and prevent them from soiling their dens. The plug is made of hair, leaves and intestinal secretions that have gone hard and dry from staying in the bear's bowels so long.

Dino-Sized Droppings

It's not just living animals that make their poopy mark. Remember paleofeces? Well, dinosaurs also left their poop behind, but in a different form — as fossilized feces. Fossils are mostly made of minerals that have gradually replaced the original flesh, bone or feces. Thanks to these remains, called **coprolites**, **paleontologists** can tell what dinosaurs ate. The poop of plant-eating dinosaurs contains the remains of leaves, seeds, pollen and even bark. Carnivores such as *Tyrannosaurus rex* left behind coprolites containing bone fragments of their unfortunate victims. Researchers have also identified something called urolite — distinctive patterns formed in the sand when dinosaurs peed on it. You can create your own homemade urolite next time you go to the beach — but if you don't want to offend fellow humans, it's probably best to simulate your pee stream with water from a pail, instead of doing it dino style.

The biggest coprolite is a *T. rex* turd named after Barnum Brown, the paleontologist who discovered the first *T. rex* fossil in 1902. Barnum (the turd, not the paleontologist) is about 67 cm (26 in.) long and 15 cm (6 in.) across.

Don't Waste Your Waste!

Dogs that roll in doo-doo and storks that gobble your feces aren't the only creatures that find ways to reuse body waste. Humans have been doing it for thousands of years.

Perhaps *because* of humans' dislike of poop, one of our first ancient uses of it was as a weapon. From the ninth century BCE up until the fourth century CE, people known as the Scythians terrorized their enemies from China to Eastern Europe with arrows rubbed in feces. Why? Because it was so unpleasant! If the arrow itself didn't kill its victim, the poop's bacteria could cause gangrene, a nasty infection that makes wounded body parts blacken and fall off and often leads to death.

Who Flung the Dung?

In medieval Europe, armies besieging their enemies' towns sometimes catapulted feces over the walls in the hope of spreading diseases. However, since medieval European settlements already had so much poop lying around in their streets, it's unclear whether flinging more of it over the walls made much difference.

While Europeans may have flung dung, the Chinese took waste warfare to a whole other level. In twelfth-century China, some potty-minded genius created an "excrement bomb." Made from hemp string and filled with gunpowder, poison and human feces, it was set on fire and catapulted, spraying the enemy with its lethal contents. Another Chinese design was the impressively named "bone-burning and bruising fire-oil magic bomb," an iron-cased weapon that exploded into fragments, flinging feces-coated pellets at the enemy.

Poop Wars

Poop has even inspired a military conflict: the guano war of 1864–1866 between Spain and its former colonies Peru, Chile, Ecuador and Bolivia. The Chincha Islands, off the coast of Peru, were covered in up to 55 m (180 ft.) of bird droppings, also known as guano. In 1840, a scientist named Justus von Liebig discovered that guano was rich in nitrogen, a fertilizer that enabled farmers to double or triple their crop yields. The guano on those islands was suddenly worth a fortune, supplying the Peruvian government with most of its annual income. So when the Spanish tried to seize the islands and profit from the poop, let's just say the feces hit the fan. The former Spanish colonies united against Spain, which was eventually forced to back off and pay for its poo just like everybody else.

Poop for Progress

While it might seem odd to go to war over bird poop, animal dung does play a surprisingly important role in the development of human civilization.

Researchers who studied prehistoric farming sites in Europe believe that humans began using animal manure as crop fertilizer 8000 years ago. Those ancient farmers might not have understood the science of manure, but they likely noticed that plants grew better in areas where animals gathered and defecated. That inspired them to experiment with collecting animal feces and using them to enrich the soil. And just in case you weren't sure about the science of manure either, here's how it works:

1. Farm animals such as cows, chickens, sheep and turkeys eat feed. Then they poop!

2. Their poop, also known as manure, is spread on the fields. The manure contains nutrients such as nitrogen, phosphorus and potassium, which help plants grow.

3. The plants produce grain, which is fed to the animals. And then the animals poop, and the cycle continues!

Happily, the animals produce so much nutrient-packed manure that farmers don't have to use as many chemical fertilizers and nobody has to fight wars over it!

Many cities have begun processing their sewage sludge, known as biosolids, for use as agricultural fertilizer. The biosolids are sterilized to remove parasites and germs. However, some scientists argue that even when sterilized, biosolids contain heavy metals, prescription drugs and potentially harmful chemicals from sewer systems that can contaminate agricultural soil and crops. Other scientists believe that the benefits of adding nutrients to the soil outweigh the risks. There are strong arguments both for and against, so no doubt the biosolid battles will continue, at least until there is more conclusive scientific evidence.

The Gold Flush

On the plus side, there's gold in them thar sewers! Researchers estimate that in a city of three million people — that's roughly the size of Toronto, Chicago or Rome — about $40 million worth of gold, silver and other precious metals are pooped out into the sewer system every year. However, except for the occasional wedding ring flushed down a toilet, most of the particles are tiny, created by manufacturing processes such as mining, electroplating and jewelry making. So far only the city of Nagano, Japan, claims to have successfully recovered any precious metal from sewage. So if you're thinking of looking for gold in your poop — well, unless you've recently swallowed a wedding ring, you're probably out of luck.

Fertilizer isn't the only thing that's made up of poop. Much of the soil that we grow our food in is actually the excrement of worms and other small creatures. So thank a worm next time you eat a big, juicy strawberry. Just remember to wash it first!

Stoop and Scoop

Poop and pee can be used for many useful things besides growing greens or giving your enemies gangrene. As filthy as European cities were in centuries past, one kind of dung you wouldn't see in the streets was dog doo-doo. That's because some resourceful leather manufacturer discovered that pooch poo contains an enzyme that softens animal hides (remember, enzymes also help you digest your food). So people collected Fido's feces to sell to leather makers. In case you were thinking about going into the once-profitable poop-scooping business, sorry: modern leather makers use chemicals instead.

But that doesn't mean that animal waste is wasted today. In India, cow dung is used to make eco-friendly construction bricks. In Italy, a material called merdacotta (cow patties mixed with clay) is crafted into furniture, tiles, flowerpots and, appropriately, toilet bowls.

Remember the Egyptian vulture using poo as a cosmetic? Before you say "silly bird," you might want to know that there's another animal that uses excrement to make itself look more desirable: humans! Bird poop is used in **facials** and in many expensive anti-wrinkle creams, reportedly because it contains an enzyme thought to soften human skin.

Fuel from Stool!

Poop has been used as a source of energy for millennia. The ancient Egyptians lived in the desert with no forests. To keep warm, they had to burn something other than wood. Forming dung into logs and burning it for both light and heat was one solution.

Today, sewage can be converted into something called biogas, a combination of methane and **carbon dioxide** that forms as feces decompose. In 2014, a fleet of poop-powered Bio-Buses was built in England, able to carry passengers up to 300 km (186 mi.) on a single tank of fuel. The Bio-Bus produces 20 percent less carbon dioxide than conventional diesel-powered buses and can reduce air pollution by up to 97 percent. Not to be out-pooped, British inventor Brian Harper has created a streetlamp that runs on dog droppings. And there is even a feces-powered phone! Perhaps you'll be inspired to invent your own poop-powered video game!

Feces occasionally find their way into the art world. In 1938, Spanish painter Pablo Picasso used his three-year-old daughter's poo to paint an image of an apple, because he said it had a unique texture and color.

Urine Luck!

It isn't just doggie doo-doo and cow pies that can be put to work. Urine has lots of useful properties, too. In medieval times, wool was placed in vats full of stale pee, where unfortunate people called fullers stomped on it until it was soft. Urine was also used as a laundry cleaner to make whites whiter, colors brighter and remove stains. And, like dog poop, it was used to soften leather.

Before more efficient methods were developed, urine was mixed with manure and wood ash to make explosives. Ammonia from stale pee reacts with oxygen, creating **nitrates**, one of the three ingredients of gunpowder along with sulfur and charcoal.

But the distinction for grossest use of urine goes to the ancient Romans, who used the ammonia in well-aged pee to whiten their teeth. Using stinky stale urine to clean their pearly whites didn't worry the Romans, though — they had a cure for bad breath, too: burned mouse poop mixed with honey. Smile!

Fecal Foodstuffs

If you think that eating excreta is limited to small-brained creatures like ants, rabbits and beetles, guess again! One of the most expensive gourmet treats in the world is *kopi luwak*, a drink brewed from coffee beans that have been eaten and then excreted by a civet, a small catlike animal. Not to be outdone, a Canadian businessman has created a new and even more expensive taste sensation: Thai elephant dung coffee. But if you really want to break your piggy bank, try panda poop green tea. It's $35 000 a pound. For that kind of money, it might be cheaper to just buy a pet panda.

On the other hand, you may prefer your beverages in a more natural state, like the members of the All India Hindu Union, who drink cow urine to ward off illness.

Accidental Dung Dining

Despite these examples, most people don't eat excreta on purpose. But it happens *accidentally* all the time. Small amounts of animal poop find their way into our food so often that health agencies have developed standards to measure how much is acceptable. For example, the United States Food and Drug Administration allows 3 mg (0.0001 oz.) of mouse poop for 0.5 kg (1 lb.) of powdered ginger. But that's nothing compared to cocoa beans —10 mg (0.0004 oz.) of rodent droppings are allowed per 0.5 kg (1 lb.). Enjoy your hot chocolate!

Out of This World Excreta

As humans developed rocket ships and began to venture out into space, they had to boldly "go" where no one had "gone" before — to the bathroom, that is! That created problems for both scientists and astronauts.

One of the earliest dilemmas of space travel was one of the oldest problems of civilization: what to do with all that poo. In the 1960s, the system was primitive. Astronauts went to the moon and back with collection bags taped to their butts. It was an unpleasant, inefficient way to deal with nature's call. Records of the astronauts' conversations from the 1969 Apollo 10 mission reveal that a wayward turd got loose in the crew quarters' zero-gravity atmosphere and had to be plucked out of the air with a napkin.

Getting rid of the poop was another tricky issue. Between 1969 and 1972, astronauts from the six Apollo lunar missions left behind 96 bags of human waste — on the moon! Now, NASA scientists want to bring some of that waste back to Earth to see if the microbes that live in human poop have survived or mutated.

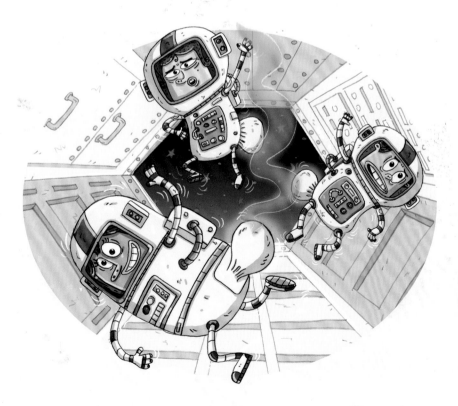

When You Wish Upon a Star

These days, astronauts no longer have to float around with bags taped to their butts, snatching wayward turds out of the air. On the International Space Station, crew members strap themselves to a toilet that uses a giant vacuum-like device to suck their poop into a storage canister. The canister is eventually jettisoned from the space station, which orbits Earth at an altitude of about 400 km (250 mi.). Upon falling about 320 km (200 mi.) down into the **mesosphere**, where gases are thick enough to cause friction, the feces burn up with a fiery, shooting star–like effect. According to NASA, during his year in space, astronaut Scott Kelly produced 82 kg (180 lb.) of poop. Considering that the average meteor weighs 2 g (0.07 oz.) or less, that's a lot of lightshow for one person!

Pretty as that sight may be, NASA-supported researchers are working on ways to use astronaut feces for something more practical: a fuel cell that uses microbes to generate electricity. As bacteria feed on the poop, they pull electrons from the feces. Those electrons can then be conducted into a circuit, generating electricity. The poopy cells could power spaceship equipment, such as communications systems, instruments and those fancy vacuum toilets!

Zero G Pee

Pee might not produce celestial spectacles, but it's another reality of spaceflight. It costs $10 000 to launch 0.5 kg (1 lb.) of anything into space. On average, an astronaut drinks a little more 3.8 L (1 gal.) of water per day. At room temperature that volume of water weighs 3.8 kg (8 2/5 lb.). That means it costs about $80 000 to send one day's supply of water — for just one person — into space. Multiply that by the number of days multiple astronauts are on a mission, and you can see just how expensive the problem is. Plus, all that water takes up room that could be used for research equipment.

To solve that problem, NASA engineers developed a system that recycles urine into clean drinking water. After astronauts urinate into a cup connected to a vacuum device, the pee is directed into a spinning drum that extracts the water vapor. It then goes through multiple filters to remove impurities, and finally, it's heated and injected with oxygen to remove any remaining contaminants. It might sound disgusting, but according to Canadian astronaut Chris Hadfield, it is "purer than most of the water that you drink at home." Who knows? Perhaps when gourmets get tired of panda-poop tea and brewed elephant dung, recycled astronaut pee will become the next luxury beverage sensation!

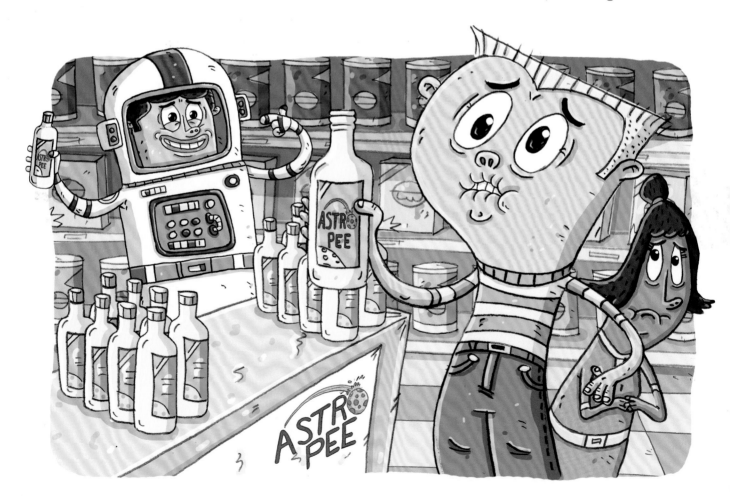

Before You Go ...

Whether it's a bus-sized cloud of poop made by a whale, or a tiny turd flung by a caterpillar, body waste can be gross — but it's a fact of life. Excreta can tell us a lot about our health and our history, and although it can be an icky problem to deal with, it can also be a valuable resource. So next time you wish upon a shooting star, remember, it might be a flaming astronaut turd. Which is fitting, if you think about it, because one of humanity's biggest dreams is to travel to other worlds, and it's possible that poop will someday help us get there!

Glossary

ammonia: an irritating, toxic chemical compound composed of nitrogen and hydrogen

antibodies: proteins that identify invaders such as bacteria or viruses and either destroy them directly or signal other parts of the immune system to attack them. Also known as immunoglobulins.

beneficial: producing good results or effects

carbohydrates: sugars, fibers and starches found in fruits, grains, vegetables and milk

carbon dioxide: a colorless, non-flammable gas known as a "greenhouse gas" because it traps heat in Earth's atmosphere

coprolites: fossilized animal poop

deterrent: something that discourages or repels

DNA (deoxyribonucleic acid): material in the cells of every living thing that contains genetic instructions determining how an organism develops and lives

E. coli: a type of bacteria that lives harmlessly in the intestines of humans and animals but can make you ill if ingested in contaminated food or water

facial: a skin care treatment for the face, typically performed in beauty salons or spas

fats: large molecules that provide energy for the body and help it absorb certain vitamins

ferment: to undergo a chemical reaction caused by organisms such as bacteria and yeast that break organic molecules down into simpler substances

fungus: a group of organisms including mushrooms as well as microbes such as yeast and mold. They feed on organic matter by dissolving it, then absorbing the nutrients.

gut microbiota: the microbes, such as bacteria, viruses and fungi, that live in the digestive systems of humans and other animals

hepatitis: a disease causing inflammation of the liver, a vital organ

hydrogen sulfide: a flammable, toxic gas that smells like rotten eggs

latrine: a toilet or a pit or trench used as a toilet

marsupial: a type of mammal that is not fully developed when born, so it is fed and protected in a pouch in its mother's body until its development is complete

mesosphere: the layer of the atmosphere that lies about 50 to 85 km (31 to 53 mi.) above Earth's surface

methane: a colorless, odorless, flammable gas

minerals: compounds such as calcium, iron and magnesium, which are important for many body functions such as keeping your bones, muscles, heart and brain healthy

molecule: the smallest amount of something you can get without breaking it down into something different. A water molecule split apart wouldn't be water anymore, it would be hydrogen and oxygen atoms.

nitrates: chemical compounds used in fertilizers and explosives

paleofeces: ancient feces that have been preserved by drying out

paleontologist: a scientist who studies the history of life on Earth based on fossil remains

parasite: an organism that lives in or on another host organism to get food and/or reproduce, harming the host in the process

proteins: nutrients made up of amino acids that are essential for making body cells and repairing existing ones

salmonella: an odorless, tasteless bacteria that causes sickness and symptoms such as diarrhea, fever and stomach cramps

taboo: forbidden or banned by a society

vitamins: substances essential for health that typically come from food or supplements, such as pills

Further Reading

Berkowitz, Jacob, and Steve Mack. *Jurassic Poop: What Dinosaurs (and Others) Left Behind.* Toronto: Kids Can Press, 2006.

Davies, Nicola, and Neal Layton. *Poop: A Natural History of the Unmentionable.* Boston: Candlewick, 2011.

Lunde, Darrin, and Kelsey Oseid. *Whose Poop Is That?* Watertown, MA: Charlesbridge, 2017.

Index

This book is dedicated to my beloved children, Mikhael and Alex, whose diapers I changed so often when they were babies that I have almost gotten over my revulsion toward poop — E.K.

To mom, June, and sister, Laurie. You've always been there to support my dreams, even when I was being a perfect little stinker. — M.S.

Published in Canada and the U.S. by Kids Can Press Ltd.
25 Dockside Drive, Toronto, ON M5A 0B5

Kids Can Press is a Corus Entertainment Inc. company

www.kidscanpress.com

The artwork in this book was drawn by pencil and completed in Photoshop.
The text is set in Bulmer.

Edited by Kathleen Keenan and Patricia Ocampo
Designed by Marie Bartholomew

Printed and bound in Shenzhen, China,
in 03/2022 by C & C Offset

CM 22 0 9 8 7 6 5 4 3 2 1

FSC
www.fsc.org
MIX
Paper from
responsible sources
FSC® C008047

Library and Archives Canada Cataloguing in Publication

Title: Poopy science : getting to the bottom of what comes out your bottom / written by Edward Kay; illustrated by Mike Shiell.

Names: Kay, Edward, author. | Shiell, Mike, illustrator.

Series: Kay, Edward. Gross science book.

Description: Series statement: Gross science

Identifiers: Canadiana 20210347538 | ISBN 9781525304132 (hardcover)

Subjects: LCSH: Feces — Juvenile literature. | LCSH: Feces — Miscellanea — Juvenile literature. | LCSH: Urine — Juvenile literature. | LCSH: Urine — Miscellanea — Juvenile literature.

Classification: LCC QP159 .K39 2022 | DDC j612.3/6 — dc23

Kids Can Press gratefully acknowledges that the land on which our office is located is the traditional territory of many nations, including the Mississaugas of the Credit, the Anishnabeg, the Chippewa, the Haudenosaunee and the Wendat peoples, and is now home to many diverse First Nations, Inuit and Métis peoples.

We thank the Government of Ontario, through Ontario Creates; the Ontario Arts Council; the Canada Council for the Arts; and the Government of Canada for supporting our publishing activity.